GEOGRAPHY OF THE WORLD

THE SACRED GANGES

By Charnan Simon

THE CHILD'S WORLD®
CHANHASSEN, MINNESOTA

The Child's World

Published in the United States of America by The Child's World®
PO Box 326, Chanhassen, MN 55317-0326
800-599-READ
www.childsworld.com

Photo Credits: Cover/frontispiece: Craig Lovell/Corbis.
Interior: Art Archive/Picture Desk: 17; Corbis: 5 (Tiziana and Gianni Baldizzone),
9 (Eric and David Hosking), 11 (Stuart Westmorland), 13 (Roger Wood), 14
(Bob Krist), 15 (Ric Ergenbright), 18 (Bojan Brecelj), 24 (Amit Bhargava); Chris
Lisle/Corbis: 4, 6; Magnum Photos: 26 (Ian Berry), 27 (Raghu Rai); Ferdinando
Scianna/Magnum Photos: 21, 22.

The Child's World®: Mary Berendes, Publishing Director

Editorial Directions, Inc.: E. Russell Primm, Editorial Director; Melissa McDaniel,
Line Editor; Katie Marsico, Associate Editor; Judi Shiffer, Associate Editor and Library
Media Specialist; Matthew Messbarger, Editorial Assistant; Susan Hindman, Copy
Editor; Sarah E. De Capua and Lucia Raatma, Proofreaders; Marsha Bonnoit, Peter
Garnham, Terry Johnson, Olivia Nellums, Chris Simms, Katherine Trickle, and
Stephen Carl Wender, Fact Checkers; Tim Griffin/IndexServ, Indexer; Cian Loughlin
O'Day, Photo Researcher; Linda S. Koutris, Photo Selector; XNR Productions, Inc.,
Cartographer

The Design Lab: Kathleen Petelinsek, Design and Page Production

Library of Congress Cataloging-in-Publication Data
Simon, Charnan.
  The sacred Ganges / by Charnan Simon.
    p. cm. — (Geography of the world series)
  Includes index.
  ISBN 1-59296-338-2 (alk. paper)
  1. Ganges River (India and Bangladesh)—Juvenile literature. I. Title. II. Series.
  DS485.G25S46 2004
  915.4'1—dc22   2004003719

TABLE OF CONTENTS

CHAPTER ONE

THE COURSE OF THE RIVER

The Ganges is India's most beloved river. It nourishes a fertile plain that feeds hundreds of millions of people. For even more people, the Ganges is considered a holy river. To these followers of the Hindu faith, the Ganges is the earthly home of the goddess Ganga.

Followers of the Hindu faith worship along the banks of the Ganges in Hardwar, India. Hindus believe that Hardwar is one of the seven holiest places in the world.

Some 850 million people worship the Ganges as a sacred river.

The Ganges begins high in the Himalayas of northwest India. The river starts out as a trickle of melted ice from the huge Gangotri Glacier. At first, this stream is known as the Bhagirathi River. It races down, down, down the mountains, slicing through sharp canyons and tumbling over waterfalls. When it reaches the village of Devprayag, the Bhagirathi meets the Alaknanda River. Once these two rivers join, they are known as the Ganges.

After dropping some 13,000 feet (4,000 meters) in just 125 miles (201 kilometers), the Ganges passes the town of Hardwar and enters a broad, flat plain. The rich, fertile farmland of the Ganges plain stretches almost 750 miles (1,200 km) across northern India. But the Ganges itself shrinks to a feeble stream at Hardwar. Most of its water has been directed into the Upper Ganges Canal near Hardwar. It is not until the Ganges is joined by several of its major **tributaries**—including the Yamuna, Ghaghar, Son, and Gandak rivers—that it becomes a mighty river again.

Beyond the city of Patna, the Ganges is so wide that you cannot see across it! The river continues its slow journey into the country of Bangladesh. Now it is joined by its largest tributary, the mighty Brahmaputra River, and later by the Meghna River. In Bangladesh, its name is officially the

THE UPPER GANGES CANAL

The Upper Ganges Canal redirects water from the Ganges River to 500 miles (800 km) of channels that carry the water to fields. The canal took 12 years to build. When it opened in 1854, it was the largest irrigation system in the world.

*Boats cruise along the Ganges River **Delta** in Bangladesh. In size, Bangladesh is a little smaller than the state of Wisconsin.*

Padma River, but many people still call it the Ganges.

As the river nears the Indian Ocean it slows down and drops the **sediment** it has carried from the mountains. Over thousands of years, this sediment has built up to form a huge triangle of land called a delta. The Ganges Delta is an ever-changing landscape of sandbars and islands, with a maze of river channels flowing in and around them. In an area called the Sundarbans, these muddy islands are covered with dense thickets of twisty mangrove trees. The Ganges Delta covers some 50,200 square miles (130,000 sq km). It is the largest river delta in the world.

At last, the Ganges pours into the Bay of Bengal, an arm of the Indian Ocean. It has traveled more than 1,560 miles (2,510 km) on its journey from the mountains to the sea.

THE HUGLI RIVER

The Hugli River is sometimes called the Ganges River's second mouth. For thousands of years, the Ganges joined the Hugli before it flowed into the Bay of Bengal. In the 12th century, the course of the Ganges changed. Now the Ganges flows eastward into Bangladesh. But some of its water still flows through the Hugli, which marks the western edge of the huge, fan-shaped Ganges Delta.

CHAPTER TWO

PLANTS AND ANIMALS

Not many plants or animals live near the Ganges River's source. It is too cold and snowy in the high Himalayas to support much life. Farther down the mountains, mahseer, catfish, and snow trout

At their highest point, the wintry Himalayas rise more than 29,000 feet (8,839 m).

swim in the chilly water. Hardy shepherds watch over herds of grazing sheep, goats, and yaks. Many trees have been chopped down for housing and fuel, but forests of pine, fir, and sweet-smelling cedar remain. Villagers are careful to avoid the Himalayan

Male jungle fowl typically weigh between 10 and 12 pounds (4.5 and 5.4 kilograms).

black and brown bears that roam these forests.

In the foothills of the Himalayas, tall grasses and bamboo groves mingle with the trees. Jackals and hyenas may lurk in the shadows, and wild water buffalo still present a danger. Pheasants, peacocks, and jungle fowl—wild ancestors of barnyard chickens—search for food in the underbrush.

Once, the Ganges plain was home to thousands of large animals such as lions, tigers, cheetahs, leopards, and rhinoceroses. Sadly, many of these animals are now endangered. People have chopped down forests, hunted animals, and overfished the river. The Indian government is working to protect its remaining wildlife. National parks offer refuge to many endangered species.

A map of the Ganges River

Scientists estimate that fewer than 3,000 Bengal tigers currently live in the wild.

FISHING-CATS
The fishing-cats of Bangladesh love to fish! They are the only member of the cat family with slightly webbed paws. Their double layer of fur keeps them dry as they fish for dinner.

The Ganges Delta in Bangladesh is also home to magnificent wildlife, including tigers, leopards, elephants, wild boar, and deer. But again, humans have damaged **habitats** and hunted so intensely that many animals are now endangered.

One spectacular animal, the royal Bengal tiger, thrives in the wet, marshy Sundarbans. Although most tigers don't like water, royal Bengals have adapted to it. They have learned to swim and even eat fish, a food most tigers avoid. Scientists believe that fewer than 300 royal Bengal tigers live in the wild in the Sundarbans. They—and the many crocodiles that lurk in the shadowy waters—present a threat to humans in the area. Every year, between 20 and 30 people, mostly fishermen, are killed by these animals.

The Sundarbans are filled with fish—both freshwater and saltwater. This area is a tidal marsh, which means that seawater flows in during high tides and out during low tides. One very unusual fish in the Sundarbans is the mudskipper. Mudskippers don't need water to survive. When the tide flows out, mudskippers "walk" around on their tails. They can even climb trees by holding on with their fins!

THE GANGES RIVER DOLPHIN

The endangered Ganges River dolphins live only in the Ganges River. These dolphins are blind. They travel on their sides, dragging one fin along the river bottom to find fish, clams, and shrimp to eat. Dams and pollution have damaged their natural habitat, and fishermen have killed them for their oil and blubber.

CHAPTER THREE

THE GANGES, PAST AND PRESENT

P eople have lived along the Ganges for thousands of years. The earliest people in the area were the Harappan. They lived along the river in small farming settlements from about 2000 B.C. to 1750 B.C.

Around 1500 B.C., a group of people from central Asia known as the Aryans moved into the Ganges plain. At first, the Aryans lived by farming. Gradually, their small villages grew larger. They began trading with people in other parts of India, Southeast Asia, Africa, and the Middle East. They developed two of India's major religions, Hinduism

The remains of these ancient Harappan granaries are located in Pakistan.

This Hindu temple in the Indian town of Thanjavur dates back to the 11th century.

HINDUISM

Today, some 81 percent of the people in India are Hindu. The religion was born in the Aryan civilizations on the banks of the Ganges in about 1500 B.C., but its roots may go back even further. Hindus everywhere consider the Ganges a holy river.

and Buddhism. In time, Aryan trading centers developed into kingdoms.

The most important early Aryan kingdom was the Mauryan empire, which ruled from about 320 B.C. to 187 B.C. At its peak, the Mauryan city of Pataliputra, on the banks of the Ganges, was home to about 450,000 people!

Later came the Gupta empire, which lasted from about A.D. 300 to 500. During this period, beautiful cities and great universities were founded. Northern India became a center of learning, medicine, and the fine arts.

During the Gupta empire, these ruins in Uttar Pradesh, India, were artfully designed stone walls.

Over the next 500 years, the Aryan civilization faded away. Armies from surrounding countries overran the area, attracted by the rich farmland of the Ganges plain.

By the 1500s, central Asian people called the Moguls had conquered northern India. They brought with them their own religion, Islam. The Moguls ruled for more than 300 years, supporting their empire by trading wheat and rice grown along the Ganges.

Also beginning in the 1500s, Europeans were growing more interested in India. Merchants of many nationalities—French, Portuguese, Dutch, and British—competed for India's valuable spice and tea trade. Eventually, a British company called the East India Company won control of much of India. In 1858, India became an official **colony** of Great Britain.

For almost 100 years, India—and the Ganges River plain— remained in British hands. But many Indians were not happy under British rule. They wanted their country back. Beginning in the 1920s, a man named Mohandas (Mahatma) Gandhi led India's struggle for independence. Gandhi didn't believe in fighting and wars. Instead, he believed in **civil disobedience.** Gandhi urged his fellow Indians to stop working for British companies and to stop shopping at British stores. He encouraged them to refuse to attend British schools or pay British taxes.

Mahatma Gandhi lived from 1869 to 1948. He is famous for peacefully liberating India from British rule.

Gandhi's ideas worked. In 1947, India won its independence from Great Britain. The country was divided into two nations, India and Pakistan. Most people in India were followers of the Hindu faith. Most people in Pakistan were followers of Islam. In 1971, part of Pakistan split off to become the country of Bangladesh. Today, the Ganges Delta is located in Bangladesh.

CHAPTER FOUR

A USEFUL RIVER

Throughout history, most people living on the Ganges plain have been farmers. The soil is rich, but farms are small. Many families can barely grow enough to feed themselves. Young people often leave home and move to nearby cities. The money they earn working

Not far from the banks of the Ganges, an Indian farmer tends to his livestock. The land surrounding the river is fertile, but many farmers live in poverty.

in offices and factories helps support the rest of the family back on the farm.

One city that young people move to is Kanpur. Large factories in Kanpur turn out foods, chemical **fertilizers,** military equipment, and leather goods. Water from the Ganges helps run these factories—but the factories themselves pollute the river.

THE GREEN REVOLUTION
Northern India has often suffered from food shortages. Today, farmers are using new types of rice and wheat to grow more crops. This "Green Revolution" means that fewer people go hungry. But the new crops need costly chemical fertilizers and weed killers. Not all Indian farmers can afford these chemicals. And when the chemicals drain into the Ganges, they pollute the river.

Allahabad is another large, modern city on the Ganges plain. Allahabad is surrounded by fields of wheat, rice, and other crops. The city has huge warehouses for storing farm produce and is an important trading center.

For hundreds of years, the Ganges was an important shipping route. But when the Upper Ganges Canal opened in 1854, much of the river's water was diverted. Large boats can no longer travel upstream beyond the city of Patna. Today, people along the Ganges use roads and railroads to ship their goods. Only in the delta is the river important for transportation. In Bangladesh, near the swampy mouth of the Ganges, boats are by far the best way of getting from place to place!

The Ganges is a useful way to travel in Bangladesh. But the river can also be a source of great misery. In winter, when little rain falls, the delta river channels shrink. The land turns dry and cracked. In summer, melting snow and heavy rains flood the delta, turning Bangladesh into an inland sea. Violent storms called cyclones blow in from the Bay of Bengal. Sometimes huge tidal waves pour into the already-flooded delta. Hundreds of thousands of people have drowned in these floods over the years, and tens of millions have lost their homes. Today, the Bangladesh government has developed an early warning system and has built cyclone shelters to help protect its people. But very little can be done to save crops and homes.

HELPFUL FLOODS

Floods can be helpful as well as harmful. When flood-waters withdraw, they leave behind rich sediment that is good for growing crops. Without this sediment from the Ganges, farmers in Bangladesh would have to use expensive fertilizers.

CHAPTER FIVE

PEOPLE ALONG THE RIVER

The Ganges River area is one of the most crowded places in the world. About 350 million people live along the Ganges—that's one out of every 20 people on earth!

Many families along the Ganges have no running water. They depend on the river for everything—their drinking water, their cooking water, and their bathing water. They wash their clothes and their animals in the Ganges. They use the river to dispose of their garbage. For these people, the Ganges really does mean life.

Do you think people only visit rivers to fish or go swimming? Residents along the Ganges use the water for everything from laundry to bathing.

Hindus believe that the Ganges once flowed in heaven, and that the river now has sacred powers on earth.

The Ganges is especially important to India's 850 million Hindus. Hindus believe that all water on earth originally came from the goddess Ganga. The Ganges River gets its name from this goddess. For Hindus, Ganges water is sacred. It has the power to heal illness and purify souls. Every Hindu hopes to visit the Ganges and bathe in it at least once. They believe the goddess Ganga will wash away their sins as she washes the dirt from their bodies.

Hindus who are lucky enough to live next to the Ganges can bathe in the river easily and often. Other Hindus make special trips to sacred spots along the river, where they bathe, pray, and drink the holy water. Providing these people with food and shelter is a major industry along the Ganges.

For Hindus, the most important city on the Ganges is Varanasi, "the city of light." This ancient, holy city has been a center of Hindu religion and learning for thousands of years. Scholars come to study at the university. Artists, dancers,

and musicians come to learn from Hindu masters. Millions of people visit Varanasi every year to bathe in the Ganges and drink its holy water. Millions more hope to die in Varanasi, or at least have their ashes scattered on the river there.

In India and Bangladesh, religious beliefs are an important part of everyday life. The Ganges is sacred only to Hindus. But the river has always been valued by people who practice Buddhism and Islam as well. Buddhist and Islamic shrines, temples, mosques, forts, and palaces line the river. Tourists from around the world visit the Ganges to see these sacred and historic sites.

CHAPTER SIX

LOOKING TO THE FUTURE

The Ganges plays a vital role in the lives of hundreds of millions of people in India and Bangladesh. Unfortunately, like many rivers today, the Ganges has become polluted.

Leather factories in Kanpur and clothing factories in Bangladesh pour poisonous chemicals into the river. These chemicals kill fish and

A sewage plant in Uttar Pradesh releases waste into the Ganges. Because the Ganges is so important to the people who live along its shores, it is essential to put an end to pollution.

plants. They make the water unsafe for drinking and cooking. The people of Kanpur and Bangladesh need clean water. But they also need the jobs provided by factories.

Cities, too, pour garbage into the river. India and Bangladesh are poor, crowded countries. Their cities are growing too fast for their sewage systems to keep up. As much as a billion liters of human waste flow into the Ganges every day. New water treatment plants must be built to clean this waste.

Individuals also pose problems. People wash themselves and their cattle in the river as part of Hindu custom. They throw the ashes of their dead loved ones into the water. Poor people cannot afford to have the bodies of their dead loved ones cremated, or burned. They often simply throw the dead bodies into the Ganges. It is not unusual to see people washing and brushing their teeth in the river, as dead bodies and garbage float past and human waste is pumped in nearby.

Other environmental problems also threaten the Ganges. Forests high in the Himalayas have been chopped down for fuel and lumber. Without tree roots to hold the soil in place, huge amounts of sediment are swept into the Ganges and down to the delta. The sediment fills up the river channels in the delta, making them shallower and more likely to flood.

Then there are the dams. Dams can be useful for storing water, producing power,

Villagers in Bangladesh watch helplessly as floodwaters flow past their homes. Flooding of the Ganges is sometimes helpful to farmers whose crops require large amounts of water, but it is often destructive as well.

preventing floods, and watering farmland. But dams also interrupt a river's natural flow. And when a river such as the Ganges flows through more than one country, disagreements arise. When India built the Farakka Dam in the 1970s, Bangladesh

Workers construct the Tehri Dam in the foothills of the Himalayas.

accused the country of trying to "steal" water from the Ganges.

There are no easy answers to the problems of the Ganges River. The governments of India and Bangladesh are looking for a peaceful way to share the river's water. They are planting new trees and making new laws to prevent pollution. They are working to build new water treatment plants and to educate people about keeping the river clean. They are studying new ways to control floods and provide better irrigation. It is hard work—but it will be worth it if the Ganges can be saved.

Glossary

bacteria (bak-TIHR-ee-uh)
Bacteria are tiny life-forms that are too small to see. Some bacteria in the Ganges may help destroy germs.

channels (CHAN-uhlz) Channels are the beds of streams or rivers. Rivers sometimes separate into two or more channels.

civil disobedience (SIV-il diss-uh-BEE-dee-uhnss) Civil disobedience is the act of peacefully refusing to obey the government and is used to affect change in a nonviolent manner. Mahatma Gandhi practiced civil disobedience.

colony (KOL-uh-nee) A colony is a settlement or country controlled by a faraway nation. India became a British colony in 1858.

delta (DEL-tuh) A delta is the flat land at the mouth of a river. Deltas are made up of sediment that has been carried downstream by the river.

fertilizers (FUR-tuh-lize-urz)
Fertilizers are substances put on fields to make crops grow better. Chemical fertilizers pollute the Ganges.

habitats (HAB-uh-tats) Habitats are places where a certain kind of plant or animal naturally lives. Many animals that once lived on the Ganges plain have lost their habitat.

irrigation (ihr-uh-GAY-shun)
Irrigation is using pipes and canals to bring water to fields. The Ganges provides irrigation for nearby farms.

sediment (SED-uh-muhnt)
Sediment is small pieces of dirt and rocks that are carried away by a river and then sink to the river bottom. Sediment from the Ganges River has made fertile land in the delta.

tributaries (TRIB-yuh-ter-eez)
Tributaries are smaller streams or rivers that flow into a larger river. The Ganges's major tributaries include the Yamuna and the Brahmaputra.

A Ganges River Almanac

Names: Ganga River and Padma River

Extent
    Length: 1,550 miles (2,500 km)
    Width: Often, too wide to see across
    Depth: Not determined

Continent: Asia

Countries: Bangladesh and India

Major tributaries: Alaknanda, Bhagirathi, Brahmaputra, Gandak, Ghaghar, Meghna, Son, and Yamuna (India)

Major cities: Allahabad, Kanpur, Kolkata, Patna, and Varanasi (India)

Major languages: Nearly 400 languages are spoken. English is used for business. Hindi is the major official language. These languages are also recognized by the government: Assamese, Bengali, Gujarātī, Hindi, Kannada, Kashmirī, Konkani, Malayālam, Manipurī, Marātī, Nepalī, Oriyā, Punjābī, Sanskrit, Sindhī, Tamil, Telugu, and Urdū.

Parks and preserves: Gir Forest and Sundarbans (India)

Natural resources: Bauxite, chromite, coal, copper, gold, iron ore, lead, manganese, silver, and zinc

Native birds: Jungle fowl, peacocks, and pheasants

Native fish: Catfish, mahseers, mudskippers, and snow trout

Native mammals: Deer, fishing-cats, Ganges River dolphins, goats, Himalayan black and brown bears, hyenas, jackals, leopards, lions, rhinoceroses, Royal Bengal tigers, sheep, water buffalo, wild pigs, and yaks

Native reptiles: Crocodiles

Native plants: Bamboos, deodars (cedars), firs, mangroves, pines, and tall grasses

Major products: Cereal, cotton, jute, leather, rice, silk, and sugarcane

The Ganges River in the News

2,000 B.C.– 1750 B.C.	Harappan people live along the river in small farming settlements.
1500 B.C.	Groups of people known as Aryans begin to arrive in the Ganges plain from central Asia.
320 B.C.– 187 B.C.	The Mauryan empire, an Aryan kingdom, rules the area.
300 A.D.– 500 A.D.	The Gupta empire builds beautiful cities and founds great universities.
1500s	The Moguls from central Asia conquer northern India. They bring Islam to India.
1854	The Upper Ganges Canal opens.
1858	India becomes an official colony of the British Empire.
1947	India wins its independence from Great Britain. The countries of India and Pakistan win their independence.
1971	Bangladesh separates from Pakistan and becomes its own country.
1975	The Farakka Dam opens.
1985	Ganga Action Plan starts to reduce levels of pollution in the river.
1996	India and Bangladesh sign a treaty to share the waters of the Ganges River.

How to Learn More about the Ganges River

At the Library

Cumming, David. *The Ganges.* Milwaukee: World Almanac Library, 2003.

Lewin, Ted. *Sacred River.* New York: Clarion Books, 1995.

Pipes, Rose. *Rivers and Lakes.* Austin, Tex.: Raintree/Steck-Vaughn, 1998.

Pollard, Michael. *The Ganges.* Tarrytown, N.Y.: Benchmark Books, 1997.

On the Web

VISIT OUR HOME PAGE FOR LOTS OF LINKS ABOUT THE GANGES RIVER:

http://www.childsworld.com/links.html

Note to Parents, Teachers, and Librarians: We routinely verify our Web links to make sure they're safe, active sites—so encourage your readers to check them out!

Places to Visit or Contact

EMBASSY OF BANGLADESH
3510 International Drive NW
Washington, DC 20008

EMBASSY OF INDIA
2107 Massachusetts Avenue NW
Washington, DC 20008

INDIA TOURISM
1270 Avenue of the Americas
Suite 1808, 18th Floor
New York City, NY 10020-1700

Index

About the Author

Charnan Simon has a BA in English literature from Carleton College and an MA in English literature from the University of Chicago. She has been an editor at both *Cricket* and *Click* magazines and has written more than 50 books for young readers. Ms. Simon lives in Madison, Wisconsin, with her husband Tom, their daughters, Ariel and Hana, Sam the dog, and Lily and Luna the cats.